WHY

STUDENTS READ BUT DON'T REMEMBER

BOOK 1

CHRISTOPHER OGAN

© 2020 Christopher Ogan

Published by LUMINA Publishing

ISBN – 978-978-987-302-9

All scripture quotations are from the King James Version of the Holy Bible unless otherwise stated.

The portions of the scriptures made **bold** are highlighted to emphasis particular areas of interest in the scriptures.

TABLE OF CONTENT

ABOUT THIS BOOK

*If I had an hour to solve a problem I'd spend
55 minutes thinking about the problem and
5 minutes thinking about solutions.*

— Albert Einstein

This book takes the Einsteinian approach to solving problems. According to Albert Einstein the genius inventor and scientist, *"If I had an hour to solve a problem I'd spend 55 minutes thinking about the problem and 5 minutes thinking about solutions"*. Einstein believed the quality of the solution you generate is in direct proportion to your ability to identify the problem you hope to solve. With that in mind, he believed a key to productivity and success was to invest your time in understanding and defining the problem as opposed to jumping right into dreaming up solutions to it.

It is also said that, *"A Problem Well-Defined is a Problem Half-Solved"*.

In this book, we are zooming in on the problem in other to find an effective and lasting solution to the problem that plague students at all academic levels: be it primary, secondary or tertiary level, hence the title **"WHY STUDENTS READ BUT DON'T REMEMBER"**.

This book is one of the *"Easy-Read Academic Success Series"* by the author. It is specially and purposely designed with large prints to make it easy to read for students of all age.

It is my hope that this book and others in this series will help you solve your academic problems, make you a better student and improve your grades.

I wish you a good reading experience.

Enjoy

Christopher Ogan

6

INTRODUCTION

The need to remember what we read is very vital and fundamental for success in all areas of life. Many students wonder why they study but do not remember what they have studied. This book will help students to understand why they read but do not remember. The essence of this book is to help students remember what they have read, by understanding how to store what they read in their brain and how to bring it out when they need it.

The brain is the information storage organ of the human body; it is the organ of memory. It's important to note that to remember anything, you have to first store it. ***You cannot get out of your brain what you have not put inside it.***

There are three storage levels in the brain and each storage level determines what you can remember and for how long. This is what many students do not know and miss out in their study. Interestingly, the act of storage of information in the brain is a voluntary and conscious thing that we have control over.

Reading to remember has to do with memory. But what is memory? Memory is the ability of an organism to record information about things or events with the facility of recalling them later at will.

It can also be seen as the ability to recall or recognize previous experience, which is the encoding, consolidating & retrieval of information gotten from our 5 senses.

It's important to understand how the brain works to store, retrieve or remember informations. This understanding is fundamental for success in any endeavour. Without this knowledge you can keep learning new things and never remember them, when you need them. And that is the beginning of failure because ***Failure to remember what we study is the beginning of failure.***

Three things influence the life of man including our ability to remember things. The three things include.

- God,
- Nature/Natural forces and
- Supernatural forces.

If we are able to harness these three forces to our advantage we would be able to have a good memory and remember things quickly. We need to harness this three forces to our advantage if we must read and remember what we read.

In the light of the above, this book will be divided into three sections to see how the different forces influence our memory or our ability to read and remember.

1. Natural or human perspective
2. Supernatural or Spiritual perspective
3. God the Creators perspective

11

Chapter ONE

NATURAL (HUMAN) PERSPECTIVE

*Under this perspective we would see that **Students do not remember what they study because they do not properly or effectively store what they read in their brain,** and this is often because they do not even know how the brain works to store the information they read, and what they need to do for the brain to effectively store what they read.*

The natural forces includes the inherent nature of man and other natural factors. Understanding the human nature and the natural workings of the human body especially the organ concerned with remembering things, otherwise called the organ of memory or the **brain,** will help us to know how to flow with nature in other to remember the thing we study.

Understanding how a thing work is essential for enjoying the best of that thing. To enjoy the best of any device we must understand how it works. The brain is a very powerful tool that if we are able to understand how it works and use it to our advantage we would be able to achieve success with ease.
To understand how the brain works and how things are stored in the brain, we need to understand the following.

1. The PRINCIPLES of memory.
2. The FORMS of memory storage and
3. The STAGES of memory creation.

HOW TO READ TO REMEMBER

INTRODUCTION

To remember anything you have to store it first in your brain.
You cannot get out of your brain what you have not put inside it.

THE PRINCIPLE

THE PRINCIPLE OF MEMORY

The principle of memory is what is called the principle or law of repetition. ***Repetition they say is the mother of learning"***. Repetition effectually transfers information from the short-term memory (which has a limited capacity) to long-term memory (which is unlimited in both capacity and duration.)

Repetition is simply the act of doing, saying, writing, or reading something over and over again. Without repetition nothing can be effectively stored in our long term memory and whatever we cannot store in our long term memory we cannot remember easily. To learn anything in life we must engage the principle of repetition.

The principle of repetition is fundamental for academic success and for success in any area.

HOW TO READ TO REMEMBER

1

THE PRINCIPLE

To store what we read
in our memory
we must memorise or
meditate on what
we read.

HOW THE BRAIN STORES INFORMATION

FORMS OF MEMORY STORAGE

There are three main forms of memory storage.

1. Sensory memory,
2. Short-term memory, and
3. Long-term memory.

Memories are generated through what we perceive with our five senses, the eyes, ear, nose, mouth and skin. Once a memory is generated by perception, this information goes to our brain and into the cells of the brain, called "neurons". The information is first kept in our short-term memory, which can hold only 7 to 9 items averagely for about 15 to 30 seconds.

1. SENSORY MEMORY

This memory is the memory that we can remember immediately after receiving a stimulus from any of the senses. Sensory memory is not consciously controlled; it allows individuals to retain impressions of sensory information after the original stimulus has ceased.

2. SHORT TERM MEMORY

Short-term memory is also known as working memory. ***It can hold only about 7 to 9 items, for an average of about 20 seconds***. However, items can be moved from short-term memory to long-term memory via processes like rehearsal or repetition. The more we read an information or use an information repeatedly, the more likely it is for it to be moved and stored in the long-term memory, or to be "retained" in the brain. ***An example of rehearsal is when someone gives you a phone number verbally and you say it to yourself repeatedly until you can write it down.*** If someone interrupts your rehearsal by asking a question, you can easily forget the number, since it is only being held in your short-term memory.

3. LONG TERM MEMORY

Long-term storage can hold an indefinitely large amount of information and can last for a very long time, sometimes even a lifetime.
To store information in our long-term memory we simply repeat the information in our brain in a loop till it goes into our long-term memory system for permanently storing, managing, and retrieving information for later use.

Storing information in this memory is what determines what we can remember as well as our level of success.

Repetition is the key to storing what we study in our long-term memory. Many students miss it at this point; they do not store what they read in their long-term memory. This is the reason they cannot remember what they have read and understood. Many students just read a book, understand it and after that they close the book and they do not read it for the next one week. I tell you, that is a waste of your precious reading time, we must make conscious efforts to remember what we have read and understood. And that is why we don't just have reading time; we must also have memorisation time. After reading and understanding what you read, we must set out time to memorise what we have read and understood.

HOW MEMORIES ARE GENERATED

STAGES OF MEMORY CREATION

1.   Perception,
2.   Encoding,
3.   Storage (Consolidation) and
4.   Retrieval

1. PERCEPTION

The creation of a memory begins with its perception: The registration of information during perception occurs in the brief sensory stage that usually lasts only a fraction of a second. It's your sensory memory that allows a perception such as a visual pattern, a sound, or a touch to linger for a brief moment after the stimulation is over.

2. ENCODING

Encoding is the first step in creating a memory. It's a biological phenomenon, rooted in the senses, that begins with perception from the five senses, that is, what we hear, see, speak, touch or smell. It's important to note that in school we learn through three major senses, which include seeing, hearing and writing. ***Note that when you read out loud, your three senses are at work and when you write as you read out loud your four senses are at work.*** This is why it's easier to remember something we read out loud.

Explaining something you are learning, for example, stores the information into what is called the semantic memory, while the act of speaking out loud stores the information in your auditory memory. In one practice, you can develop multiple methods of storing and retrieving information! The same concept applies when listening to someone and jotting down notes.

3. STORAGE OR CONSOLIDATION.

We see that you can read and actually not store what you read in your long-term memory. This is where a lot of students miss it. They read and understand but they do not store what they understand into their long-term memory. To store what we read to our long-term memory in other to remember them when we need them, we must engage the principle of repetition.

Repetition is reading out loud (audibly) repeatedly with our mouth.

When you repeat things you create many more neural pathways. ***Repetition helps you to form multiple neural pathways, meaning your brain (or the information you have stored) has more than one road to travel when you want to retrieve the information.***

Another way we store information to our brain store is through memorization. Memorization is reading in our mind, it is learning by heart or committing what we have read to memory; this is actually the part that stores what you have read in your memory. Memorizing what we have read is very important because it consolidates (solidifies or strengthen) the stored information.

4. RETRIEVAL/RECALL

Retrieval of information has to do with trying to remember what you have read. It is making conscious effort to remember what we have read. Retrieval also has to do with meditating on what we have read and to some extent involves memorization.

Meditation is thinking SERIOUSLY about something in our mind. This serves two purposes; it helps you to store information and also to retrieve stored information. Meditation serves as a retrieval as well as a storage mechanism.

Reading without memorizing or meditating on what you read will always leave you stranded in an exam condition. This is what happens when people say; they forgot all that they have read.

This phase is very important because it helps you to know what has been stored into your memory. It's like examining yourself before the examination. Whatever you can get out of your brain at this stage, you will comfortably be able to retrieve it during an exam.

In concluding this chapter it's IMPORTANT TO NOTE that when studying to remember we must store the informations in little bits.

To store informations you want to remember to your brain, you must store them in bits. Break them into little bits before storing them. Memorize and meditate on what you read in bits and chunks. You cannot store large information at once. You must break them into brain digestible bits. Storing information into your brain storage is similar to storing food to your stomach storage. You don't eat all the food in your plate at once, you eat them spoon after spoon and before you know it, it's all in there. You must store things to your brain in bits and chunks. Start with the subtopics, headings, summaries, and important points etc. Looking at this book for instance, to remember everything in this book you start by breaking it into the different subtopics, what is memory, the principle of memory, the forms of memory and the stages of memory. Then you go on to store the major informations under the subtopics, for the forms of memory (you store the sensory, short term and long term memory), for the stages of memory (you store perception, encoding, storage and retrieval). After that, you can now go on to store the details of what happens under each subtopic. Remember you store this information by repeatedly reciting them. By doing this you will discover that you can remember everything written in this book, you can even remember the right location or chapter to find any information. So you notice that you will go through a ***"Read–Repeat–Memorise, Read–Repeat–Memorise loop"***.

It's important to note that without memorisation there is no memory. *Without memorisation there will be nothing to remember.* Memory comes through memorisation. **Memorisation is the secret to remembering anything.** A student who does not memorise what he reads can never be an excellent student.

Let me close this chapter with this true-life story that reflects the power of repetition on learning. This story is about my eight months old son. We noticed for some time that with his natural instincts he comes down from the bed or staircase hand and head first. And then we thought we should teach him how to come down backwards and leg first, so my wife taught him first and we noticed he was still coming down hands first, then I decided to teach him and still he was using his instinctive hand-first method. Then his two years eight months old big brother now taught him and still we noticed that he was still using his instinctive method. Then all of a sudden the next day we noticed to our amazement that he began to use the back and leg-first method. You can only imagine our excitement. This happened just about three days before the writing of this book so you can imagine why it had to be a part of the inspiration in this book.

Now this is a little child who cannot consciously learn things, but in an average of four repetitions he was able to learn something and store it in his memory. Now, he is only eight months old, imagine what you who has the capacity to consciously learn things achieve through repetitions.

I can tell you assuredly, that you need an average of four repetitions to store information in your long term memory. Which means as a student if you must remember what you have read in an examination, you must have read that thing repeatedly for at least four times.

You must understand that repetition is a universal law, just like the law of gravity, it applies to every human being, race, age and sex notwithstanding. The law of repetition is essential for success, you cannot achieve academic success without it. And like every other natural law, we cannot bend it to suit us, we can only align ourselves with it. I encourage you therefore, to flow with the law of repetition and achieve success with ease.
Always remember these words...

"Repetition is the mother of learning".

"A student who does not memorise or repeat what he reads can never be an excellent student."

1

REPETITION MEMORISATION MEDITATION

are the keys to remembering whatever we read.

THE SIX R'S FOR REMEMBERING THINGS

Under this topic I give you SIX R's that I believe you need, to boost your memory and remember things. These are proven principles that I have personally applied and I believe will work for any dummy who can read. I therefore introduce you to the 6 R's (RRRRRR) for remembering things. They include: REVIEW, READ, REDUCE, RECITE, REFLECT, REST.

1. REVIEW

This first "R" demands that we reexamine ourselves, refresh our memory, brush up, try to remember or recall what we had read in our last study before moving unto the area of study for the day. This REVIEW is very necessary because it helps us to know what we have successfully stored and what remains to be stored. It also helps us to consolidate the information we have stored in our long term memory. It's important to take note of what we cannot remember and go back to view them briefly before we commence our study for the day. The review process can be given about 10 to 15 minutes depending on the volume of information.

2. READ

The second "R" is the part where we spend time to read what we have chosen to study for the day. Here are some tips that will help you through this phase.

- **SKIM:** To start reading skim through the note or text briefly, taking note of the titles, subtitles and important key words. After this you go back to the beginning and read your course materials thoroughly.
- **READ ALOUD:** Reading aloud is a great way to do this as it helps information enter your long-term memory. By reading aloud you get three of your senses to work (your mouth, ear and eye) and by engaging them you create multiple pathways for the storage of the information.
- **PICTURE WHAT YOU ARE READING:** It's advisable to *picture what you are reading*. Creating a mental picture of what you are reading allows the brain to take shots of what you are reading and store them like a movie.

This mental pictures will help you to remember what you are reading.

- **MIX TOPICS:** You should also try to mix up topics during your study time, so you don't lose interest. If you feel like you've understood your material switch to something else, then come back to it later and see if you still remember it.
- **LOOK UP WORDS YOU DON'T UNDERSTAND:** Don't study without a pen, a notepad and a dictionary. Thanks to advancement in technology now we have digital dictionaries in our mobile phones. Look up words you don't understand.
- **TAKE BREAKS:** Don't forget to take breaks. Taking breaks will help you relax your mind to accommodate more information.

3. REDUCE

This is the third "R" in the series. This R demands that you reduce your course material into summaries and key points. Once you've taken notes in the course of your study, summarise them. Identify the key points, concepts and dates and then write them up in

your own words. Breaking down the information into little bits and chunks will help you to memorise information better and to store them in your brain. To achieve this with ease its often good to divide your note book into two columns; a column for your lecture notes and a column for summary or additional notes. If you are able to do this, all you have to do during your revision for examination is to focus on the summary section. This was one technique I applied during my undergraduate days and it worked for me.
Here are some tips to help you through this.

- **MARK/HIGHLIGHT TEXT:** Highlight important points, concepts and ideas. Don't highlight too much. Write questions where necessary.
- **WRITE A FEW SUMMARIES:** Write the summary of each page or paragraph at the end of each page.

4. RECITE

This fourth "R" demands that we recite the chunks or bits of information we want to store in our brain, perhaps from the key points we have summarised. This is the part where we apply the principle of repetition. This is one of the most active ways of studying and can help you to store information more securely. Practicing this fourth R helps us to store information into our long term memory. To do this effectively you should keep repeating your summarised notes aloud. This will then test your knowledge and help you discover the gaps in your memory. You can allocate time at your discretion for this section.

5. REFLECT/RECALL

This "R" which is the fifth R demands that we reflect on what we have learnt. After studying your course materials it is a good idea to reflect on what you have learnt. This process is also called the RECALL process. Repeatedly recalling information helps strengthen the connections in your brain and your memories. This is the process of taking a mock exam before the actual exam. Ask yourself questions and try to examine yourself. Some questions may include: why are these facts important? What are the important points in the passage? This will then enhance the reflective process.

It's important we examine ourselves by writing out possible examination questions from the passage. Whatever we can answer in our personal examination process, will be easy for us to answer in an examination condition. It's like taking an examination with the same questions for a second time or third time depending on how many times we examine ourselves. This part requires applying the principle of meditation and memorisation. Practicing this part consolidates the information we store in our long term memory. Here are some tips to help you through this stage.

- **DISCUSS YOUR READING WITH CLASSMATES**. Try discussing what you have read with your friends and classmates of like mind. When you explain what you have read and understood to someone, it sticks quickly and easily to the brain. It's like teaching yourself the same thing again and again. This is very vital for consolidating information in your brain. This is usually where I say you can't achieve success alone, you need a team player to achieve success. I remember how after our study, on our way home from the library, I and my friend Paul would use the long walk home to discuss what we have read. We always look forward to this time because it was time for us to show our intellectual prowess. We didn't know what we were doing then but we realised that it helped us to remember everything we read and discussed. This did not only help us to succeed but it also made our friendship bond stronger. If you don't have anyone to talk to, try talking to yourself out loud. Just the act of speaking can help you learn.

- **THINK OF OPEN ENDED QUESTIONS**: Write down some open-ended questions that might be interesting to discuss.

6. REST

The sixth "R" demands that we sleep or rest well after every day's hard work. Sleep has proven to be one of the most important elements in having a good memory. Most of our memory consolidation process occurs when we sleep, it therefore makes sense that without enough sleep we're going to struggle to remember the things we've learned. Even a short nap can improve your memory recall. The problem with many students is that, they wait until a week to the examination (or when the examination time table is out) before they start studying. They spend sleepless nights reading and hoping they will remember what they read in the exam hall, but only to discover right there in the examination hall that they cannot remember what they have read. They cannot remember because they have not spent enough time to sleep in other to store what they have read in their long term memory. Lack of good sleep has become the undoing of many students. This knowledge should help students plan their study time, as well as their resting time.

Research has shown that when memory is first recorded in the hippocampus of the brain, it's still "fragile" and easily forgotten, especially if the brain is asked to memorize more things. Napping, however, pushes memories to the neocortex, the brain's "more permanent storage," preventing them from being "overwritten."

Not only is sleep after learning a critical part of the memory creation process, but sleep before learning something new is important as well. Research has found that sleep deprivation can affect our ability to commit new things to memory and consolidate any new memories we create. In a recent sleep deprivation research by one of my colleagues it was discovered that sleep deprivation affects coordination and memory.

Now that you know the natural perspective to remembering what you read, I encourage you to apply them for your academic success.

Chapter TWO

SUPERNATURAL (SPIRITUAL) PERSPECTIVE

*Under this perspective we would see that **Students don't remember what they have read because what they store in their brain is removed or stolen by demonic forces.***

It is commonly said that the spiritual realm controls the physical realm and this is very true. It is true that the supernatural controls the natural even in our quest to study to remember. If the supernatural messes up with our natural dimension of remembering things, there is nothing we do that will make us remember what we read even when we have fulfilled all the natural conditions. It's important to note that in the spiritual realm we have the good forces and the evil forces. God and His Spirits are the good forces and Satan and his demonic evil spirits are the evil forces. The good forces help us to remember things while the evil forces make us to forget things. The Holy Spirit helps us to remember things while the devil steals what we have read from our mind and cause us to forget those things. Yes! The devil can steal the words you have read (or have been taught) from your mind and cause your to forget.

If the good forces are on your side, there is nothing the evil forces can do to you. For if God be for you who can be against you.

Let's take a look at the parable of the sower from the holy Bible...

Luke 8:5. A sower went out to sow his seed: and as he sowed, some fell by the way side; and it was trodden down, and the fowls of the air devoured it.

6. And some fell upon a rock; and as soon as it was sprung up, it withered away, because it lacked moisture.

7. And some fell among thorns; and the thorns sprang up with it, and choked it.

11. Now the parable is this: The seed is the word of God.

12. Those by the way side are they that hear; then cometh the devil, and taketh away the word out of their hearts, lest they should believe and be saved.

13. They on the rock are they, which, when they hear, receive the word with joy; and these have no root, which for a while believe, and in time of temptation fall away.

14. And that which fell among thorns are they, which, when they have heard, go forth, and are choked with cares and riches and pleasures of this life, and bring no fruit to perfection.

From the above scripture we see that there are three major ways the devil makes people to forget what they have read or have been taught.

1.   By directly stealing the word from their spirit and mind.

2.   By bringing temptations to sin their way thus preventing the word from taking root or from being stored in their mind.

3.   By distracting them with the cares, riches and pleasures of life, thus removing their focus from their study. That is why you hardly see students who are commonly called runs girls sitting down to study, they use their study time for pleasure and money. This is also the reason why students would rather use their study time to club and drink, the pleasures of life.

The first method is used to steal words before they even have the opportunity to be stored in the brain, the second method is used to prevent words that were not stolen from being stored in the brain, the third method is used to distract the focus of the target from the process of learning.

Let's focus on the first method.

*Luke 8:12. Those by the way side are they that hear; then cometh the devil, and **taketh***

away the word out of their hearts, *lest they should believe and be saved.*

Please don't say this only concerns the word of God, NO! It concerns every learning process that requires words, and almost everything in life is learnt through words (either spoken or written). It applies to every area of life. It applies to all word learning processes, whether you are learning (training) to be a doctor, engineer, or whether you are in the arts, sciences, social sciences, theology, whatever field of study it is, it doesn't matter, the demonic spiritual fowls can steal those words. However it's important to note that these demonic fowls are more attracted to steal spiritual words (the seed of the word of God) than other words. That however does not mean that they cannot steal words other than spiritual words. They often steal words other than spiritual words when they have a target, for instance when a witch or any demonic being wants to hinder the academic progress of someone they are targeting, they send their "word scavenging fowl spirits" to this people to steal what they read from their mind and often they wait until the exam time so that those students will be helpless after that.

These word scavenging fowl spirits are on a mission to steal words from the mind of people in other to kill their dreams and destroy their destinies. As stated earlier they go more for the word of God in the minds of the people and that is why it is very important to write what your hear in church (or in your spirit) as you study the bible so that even if it gets stolen you can read it again and again and put it back into your brain.

The devil can go into the spirit and soul of a man and steal whatever he wants. Note that the devil steals both spiritual and physical things, he steals everything steal-able including somethings as minut as a word. You may think, is it not just mere words? Don't forget that words are seeds and the growth of anything depends on the growth of that word seed. Don't forget that whatever words we learn in school is what we would apply to get jobs, start a business and succeed in life. The job, business, etc are the fruits of the word we learn in school.

So yes, the devil can go into the spirit and soul of a man to steal the words that he has stored there through the application of the natural principles of repetition.

And **this is why we must keep our spirits and soul secured.** The Holy Spirit has a way of securing our spirit and mind from the invasion of the word scavenging demonic fowls or spirits.

Proverbs 25:28. He that hath no rule over his own spirit is like a city that is broken down, and without walls.

When your spirit is not secured, you loose control of it. And when you have no control over your spirit, the devil can come in anytime and steal from your spirit, he can even pollute your spirit by depositing demonic garbage and rubbish into your spirit. This garbages can cause depression, doubt, lack of interest to study, slumber during study etc. When this happens you see that the mind of such people comes under the bondage of the evil spirits such that the spirits control it at will. At this point the mind of such a person needs to be saved. King David when his soul was being overwhelmed by depression had to ask God to deliver and save his soul.

Psalm 69:1. Save me, O God; for the waters are come in unto my soul.
14. Deliver me out of the mire, and let me not sink: let me be delivered from them that hate me, and out of the deep waters.
15. Let not the waterflood overflow me, neither let the deep swallow me up, and let not the pit shut her mouth upon me.
18. Draw nigh unto my soul, and redeem it: deliver me because of mine enemies.
20. Reproach hath broken my heart; and I am full of heaviness: and I looked for some to take pity, but there was none; and for comforters, but I found none.

The soul David was referring to here was not his soul as a being but his mind and the waters here represent demonic influences that were attacking his soul (mind) to get him depressed. One of such demonic influences was what made him to take Uriah's wife and after that he plotted the killing of Uriah so that he could have his wife all to himself (2 Samuel 11:15).

The good, gentle and caring David could not have done such an evil thing without an external demonic influence. All his plans started as a thought before they eventually became actions and all through the time of hatching this evil plan, he was influenced by demonic forces which he referred to as waters. David knew that this was not his mind but the work of the waters that had come into his mind and he had to pray to God earnestly for the salvation of his mind from this external evil spiritual influences.

When we notice that our mind is under bondage, we must quickly and earnestly seek God for the salvation of our mind, we must pray and ask God to save our mind and brain from the bondage of the Devil. How do you know your mind is under bondage? You know your mind is under the bondage of external evil forces when you don't have control over it, when we cannot tell it what to do, or when to sleep, or when to focus, or what to think. You know, when your mind is always thinking evil, sinful and negative thoughts, or when it begins to think thoughts that are unusual or unlike you, when your mind is always depressed or when you find yourself being fearful always.

We must strive to ensure that our spirit and mind is secured from every demonic influences. We must keep the fence of our mind high and intact. See what the bible says when the defence or fence round our spirit is broken.

Ecclesiastes 10:8. He that diggeth a pit shall fall into it; and whoso breaketh an hedge, a serpent shall bite him.
11. Surely the serpent will bite without enchantment; and a babbler is no better.

Serpents will come in and bite or afflict the person whose spiritual defence is broken, and you know what Serpents represent, Satan the Devil and his demonic agents, including the word scavenging fowls. From the scripture above we see that we are of the the ones that break the hedge, barrier or wall around our mind and spirit. We break our hedge when we commit sin through anger, lying, stealing or any other sin. When we sin we give place to the devil to come into our spirit and soul to steal, kill and destroy or dream, vision and destiny (Ephesians 4:23:32).

HOW TO SECURE YOUR SPIRIT FROM DEMONIC INVASION AND THEFT

You can secure your spirit and prevent word theft from your spirit. I have identified four ways to secure our spirit to prevent the devil from stealing what we have read.

1. BY SECURING THE PEACE OF GOD THROUGH PRAYER

Peace of mind is a product of prayer. When we pray and make our requests to God and thank him in return, prayer builds a shield of peace round about us. Pray for the salvation of your soul especially when you notice or feel that your soul has been held captive by the devil.

When you pray to the point that you experience peace in your heart, this peace of God forms a shield of protection around your spirit and mind, keeping every word scavenging evil spirit and bird away from your spirit.

Philippians 4:6. Be careful for nothing; but in every thing by prayer and supplication with thanksgiving let your requests be made known unto God.

7. And the peace of God, which passeth all understanding, shall keep your hearts and minds through Christ Jesus.

2. BY THE HELP OF THE HOLY SPIRIT.

The Holy Spirit in us prevents evil spirits from coming near us to steal form us. No matter the demonic invasion, even when you are asleep, your spirit is secure, no evil spirit can come in and steal from your spirit or mind. The Holy Spirit has a spiritual mechanism that keeps the Devils off your soul and spirit even when you are asleep.

Isaiah 59:19. So shall they fear the name of the LORD from the west, and his glory from the rising of the sun. When the enemy shall come in like a flood, the Spirit of the LORD shall lift up a standard against him.

3. BY STUDYING THE WORD OF GOD.

Proverbs 30:5. Every word of God is pure: he is a shield unto them that put their trust in him.

The word of God acts as a shield that protects our spirit. In truth the word of God is the blocks or bricks we use to build a fence around our spirit (Acts 20:32).

Obedience to the word of God build a shield of protection around our heart.

The word of God will help you to overcome the cares and pleasures of life.

Proverbs 6:20. My son, keep thy father's commandment, and forsake not the law of thy mother:
21. Bind them continually upon thine heart, and tie them about thy neck.
22. When thou goest, it shall lead thee; when thou sleepest, it shall keep thee; and when thou awakest, it shall talk with thee.

23. For the commandment is a lamp; and the law is light; and reproofs of instruction are the way of life:
24. To keep thee from the evil woman, from the flattery of the tongue of a strange woman.

Proverbs 4:20. My son, attend to my words; incline thine ear unto my sayings.
21. Let them not depart from thine eyes; keep them in the midst of thine heart.
22. For they are life unto those that find them, and health to all their flesh.
23. Keep thy heart with all diligence; for out of it are the issues of life.

4. BY THINKING GOOD THOUGHTS.

Proverbs 23:7. For as he thinketh in his heart, so is he: Eat and drink, saith he to thee; but his heart is not with thee.

Man is a product of his thoughts. We attract what we think. If we think evil and negative thoughts we would attract evil and negative spirits. If we think good and positive thoughts we would attract the good spirit of God.

We are encouraged by Apostle Paul to think only positive thoughts, that when we do this the peace of God will rule, protect and shield our hearts.

Philippians 4:8. Finally, brethren, whatsoever things are true, whatsoever things are honest, whatsoever things are just, whatsoever things are pure, whatsoever things are lovely, whatsoever things are of good report; if there be any virtue, and if there be any praise, think on these things.
9. Those things, which ye have both learned, and received, and heard, and seen in me, do: and the God of peace shall be with you.

If what you are thinking about does not align with the above things in the scripture, you must discard them from your thoughts and focus on these positive thoughts.

God responds to our words as well as our thoughts, if we think negative thoughts negative vibes like lack of interest to study, lack of confidence, sleepiness, doubt etc will be released into our system. But if we think positive thoughts positive energy will be released into out system that will strengthen us to study and empower us to stay focused on our study until we achieve success.

*Ephesians 3:20. Now unto him that is able to do exceeding abundantly above all that we **ask or think,** according to the power that worketh in us,*

It's important to note that **negative thoughts stiffen our mind but positive thoughts relax our mind.** When we think positive thoughts we relax our mind and make it easy for it to store and accommodate the information that we want to store.

5. BY LIVING A HOLY LIFE

Sin attracts the devil. To keep your spirit fortified you must live holy. The book of first John five verse eighteen tells us that when we keep ourselves holy the wicked one cannot touch us. Also the book of Ecclesiastes chapter ten verses eight and nine tells us that when we break the hedge (sin), a serpent (the devil) will bite and that without enchantment.

WORD OF CAUTION

Many students are quick to point fingers at demonic forces, as the main reason they cannot remember what they read, when they have not even done their part. Don't be in a hurry to point fingers at the forces of wickedness until you have done all that you should do to store and remember what you read.
First you have to be sure you have stored something in your brain before you begin to point fingers at the devil or the people in your village.

Most importantly, you now know how to overcome the influence of the evil forces against academic success, I therefore encourage you to apply the instructions herein for your success.

You are now unstoppable.

Chapter THREE

GOD THE CREATOR'S PERSPECTIVE

*In this section we would see that **Students do not remember what they read because they have not sought for the help of God, the Creator and Maker of man and the brain.***

Students must seek the help of God, they must ask God to help them remember what they read. The Lord Jesus speaking in Mathew 7:7 said he that asks receives.

Until we ask God for his help we can be born again and still not receive the help of God. We must ask for His help whenever we need it.

And how do we ask for his help as it concerns remembering what we read?

Ask God to give you the gift of the Holy Spirit.

But what has the Holy Spirit got to do with you remembering things you may ask?

Well, the Holy Spirit has everything to do with our remembering things. In truth he is the spirit that helps us to remember things that we have read and have been taught. Evil spirits make us forget things but the Holy Spirit helps us to remember things.

Hear what the Lord Jesus said about the Holy Spirit.

John 14:26. But the Comforter, which is the Holy Ghost, whom the Father will send in my name, he shall teach you all things, and **bring all things to your remembrance**, *whatsoever I have said unto you.*

The Holy Spirit shall bring all things to your remembrance...
One of the work of the Holy Spirit is to help you remember things. So if you are filled with the Holy Spirit you can ask him in an examination hall to help you remember what you have read. But remember you must have read and stored the information there first. The

Holy Spirit will not remind you what you have not stored in your brain. Therefore without storing anything in your brain, you leave the Holy Spirit with nothing to remind you of. Please don't go about thinking because you are filled with the Holy Spirit you can achieve success without reading, you will be deceiving yourself. The Holy Spirit does not work like that.

Another thing the Holy Spirit can do for you is to sharpen your brain to help you understand or comprehend things quickly and easily. That is why you need the Holy Spirit even more, because He gives you an edge over those who do not have him.

Having the Holy Spirit in us and allowing Him work in us is like operating with the mind of God. Well you can imagine the kind of exploits and success you can achieve having God-kind of mind. No wonder Paul first Corinthians two sixteen said "we have the mind of Christ". Having this mind of God is real by the help of the Holy Spirit. Paul enjoyed the mind of Christ, you too can.

The Holy Spirit is our comforter, He gives us comfort and ease when we are faced with any difficult situation. He is always there with us, waiting for us to ask for His help. Just a whisper of His name and our request will move him to act quickly on our behalf. He is God with us, He is Immanuel. He is the Spirit of Jesus Christ. He is Jesus with us in Spirit. He is always with us waiting for us to as much as whisper our desires to Him.

He is a gift of God to man. We do not receive him out of merit, we receive Him out of passion and desire. We receive Him when we thirst for Him. He is attracted to our thirst, desire and passion for Him.

Luke 11:9. And I say unto you, Ask, and it shall be given you; seek, and ye shall find; knock, and it shall be opened unto you.

10. For every one that asketh receiveth; and he that seeketh findeth; and to him that knocketh it shall be opened.

11. If a son shall ask bread of any of you that is a father, will he give him a stone? or if he ask a fish, will he for a fish give him a serpent?

12. Or if he shall ask an egg, will he offer him a scorpion?

13. If ye then, being evil, know how to give good gifts unto your children: **how much more shall your heavenly Father give the Holy Spirit to them that ask him?**

The Holy Spirit is God's good gift to man. As easy as it is for an earthly father to give bread to his biological son, that is how easy it is for God to give the Holy Spirit to His children. Think about this for a moment. Bread is the cheapest food any parent can afford, and no father including those who are evil will deny their children any food that they can afford, unless of course they cannot afford it.

However note that there must be a Father-son relationship for this gift of the Holy Spirit to be given easily and quickly to you. In other words you must be a child of God before you can qualify for this gift, you must be born again before you can enjoy this gift.

Acts 2:38. Then Peter said unto them, Repent, and be baptized every one of you in the name of Jesus Christ for the remission of sins, and ye shall receive the gift of the Holy Ghost.

Seek the Holy Spirit with your soul and with your body. Seeking the Holy Spirit with your body is preparing your body for him through water baptism by immersion.

Psalm 63:1. O God, thou art my God; early will I seek thee: my soul thirsteth for thee, my flesh longeth for thee in a dry and thirsty land, where no water is;
2. To see thy power and thy glory, so as I have seen thee in the sanctuary.

King David was thirsting for the Holy Spirit and through his thirst he received the Holy Spirit, such that the Holy Spirit spoke through him many times (Acts 1:16).

2 Samuel 23:1. Now these be the last words of David. David the son of Jesse said, and the man who was raised up on high, the anointed of the God of Jacob, and the sweet psalmist of Israel, said,
2. The Spirit of the LORD spake by me, and his word was in my tongue.

The other two forces (the natural and the supernatural forces) that influence man are under the control of God. And only He can show us how to use or operate both the natural and supernatural to our advantage. Yes! God can help you to control both forces to your advantage. People can exploit the natural forces or laws to become successful but that is only when the spiritual forces are on their side. It's important to note however that when you have God, even when the supernatural forces are against you, you will still be successful in your study and remember the things that you study.

God helps you to use both the natural forces and the supernatural forces to your advantage. God helps you to store what you have read and to remember them by enhancing, sharpening or quickening your brain to understand, retain and store information. And also by securing your mind (brain) and preventing word theft from your brain by demonic spiritual forces.

God can sharpen our brain to store, retain and remember what we study.
Pray and Ask God to sharpen your brain. The sharper your brain the easier it is for you to

remember things. And the good news is God can sharpen your brain.

We must ask for God's help. If you do not ask God for his help, the devil will use the opportunity to afflict you, your memory, your vision.

All that is written in Chapter one above is what God was teaching man in Joshua 1:8. We see God in that scripture teaching man how to harness the natural force to achieve success.

*Joshua 1:8. This book of the law shall not depart out of thy mouth; but **thou shalt meditate therein day and night**, that thou mayest observe to do according to all that is written therein: for then thou shalt make thy way prosperous, and then thou shalt have good success.*

"This BOOK of the law shall not depart out of thy mouth": This is reading aloud and applying REPETITION to ENCODE and store the information into your LONG TERM MEMORY.

"MEDITATE therein day and night": This is consolidating what you have read and trying to repeatedly remember or RETRIEVE what you have read.

"OBSERVE to do according to all that is WRITTEN THEREIN": This is putting ALL that needs to be remembered to work when you need it (eg. In exams, work place, business, academics etc). The purpose of remembering anything we study is to do it, or to put the knowledge we remember to work.

THEN COMES SUCCESS...

"Then thou shalt make thy way prosperous, and then thou shalt have good success".

GOOD SUCCESS is a product of applying all that is written above. This, is the ONLY PRINCIPLE for success.

Many students do not achieve success in their academics because they have not applied this ONE and ONLY principle for success.

This principle applies to both spiritual and physical things. In Joshua 1:8 we see God teaching man how to learn new things, how to study to remember and how to achieve good success.

There is no other way to lasting success (or what the bible calls good success), than what has been revealed above, which is the art of studying to remember. Note that, in the entire holy Bible there is only one scripture that talks about the principle of success, meaning there is no other way to success other than learning to remember and putting what you remember to use when you need it.

Guys this information is very important, you need to treat it as gold if you really want to achieve good success. I didn't know this when I was in school, I wish I knew because if I did I believe I would have performed better in my academics.

Please make the most of this information.

I hope to see you successful.

CONCLUSION

God the Creator of all things controls both the natural and the supernatural forces and can give a level of this control to those who are loyal and obedient to Him. God can sharpen our brain and make us super-intelligent.

In concluding this book, let me share with you this personal testimony to validate the truth that God can sharpen your brain and make you super-intelligent. I remember in my first year as an undergraduate student I had about three F's which badly impacted on my CGPA, which at the end of the day resulted in me having a third class grade after my year one. When I saw the result I wept and wept and wept, knowing that it was not a reflection of my ability. However, amidst this failure one good thing happened to me at the end of my first year which unknown to me, was later going to be my ticket to success. Guess what this wonderful thing was that happened to me? Well, I got born again. Yes! born again. This experience changed my life. If I had not become born again at that time, I would not have discovered the secret that empowered me to graduate with a good grade after such a failure in my year one. In one of the church meetings those days after my failure in year one I caught a word which quickened, enhanced and transformed my mind and made me super-intelligent. That word I caught is what is written in Isaiah chapter forty one verse fifteen.

Isaiah 41:15. Behold, ***I will make thee a new sharp threshing instrument having teeth: thou shalt thresh the mountains, and beat them small,*** *and shalt make the hills as chaff.*
16. Thou shalt fan them, and the wind shall carry them away, and the whirlwind shall scatter them: ***and thou shalt rejoice in the LORD, and shalt glory in the Holy One of Israel.***

The understanding I caught from this scripture that day was that, God will sharpen my mind (brain) such that I will understand every difficult course and those that are less difficult will be a work over for me. This scripture became my watchword, I kept speaking it and meditating on it. Now this scripture came to pass speedily such that when my fellow students who have difficulty understanding a particular course ask how they can get to understand the course, they would be asked to go and get a photocopy of my notebook, that as soon as they read it, they will understand the course. That was how my notebook became hotcake in my department and faculty. It was such that even after I left the university students who didn't even know me began to photocopy my notebook as a study material for easy understanding. Now, can I shock you a little? I graduated and left the university in 2007 but do you know that in 2019 (twelve years after) I saw one of my classmates in those days who is now a lecturer using a photocopy of my undergraduate notebook to teach students in 2019. Isn't that amazing? Now that is how powerful the word I caught that day was.

Now, at the time I caught this word at the end of my first year, a spirit inside me (which I believe is the Holy Spirit) kept telling me that, if I graduate with a grade less than a second class upper, it would be like I didn't go to school. What? With these words ringing in my spirit I sat down and projected the grades I will need to have for me to be able to graduate with a second class upper. So I began working on it and with the help of God and His word I graduated with a second class upper to the amazement of my lecturers who knew my CGPA in my first year. Most of the students who were ahead of me with good second class upper grades in our first year dropped in their CGPA and many could not even make it to a second class upper grade in our final year. Now, do you see why I said, getting born again was the best thing that happened to me in my first year?

Now that is not all, after my graduation I got an opportunity to study abroad in the United Kingdom on a scholarship and part of the requirement was that the beneficiary must have a second class upper. And that was how God supernaturally prepared me and arranged an opportunity for me to go and study abroad for my Masters degree. Now imagine that I didn't graduate with a second class upper, I would have lost the opportunity when it came stirring at me in the face. This is what is often said, *"when preparation meets opportunity success is born"*. Many of my classmates had the opportunity but they lost it because they were not prepared for it. At that time I never thought I could travel abroad to study but by the help of God and following His leading I was able to prepare for what lie ahead for me.

If you have read through this personal true life testimony of mine, I would like you to be motivated by these words. I would like you to imbibe two things from all these that I have written. Firstly, if you are not born again please get born again and secondly, strive to graduate with at least a second class upper grade.

So many opportunities await you in the future, you may not look like someone that can go abroad to study or live there at the moment but I tell you, if you prepare yourself for it, you will find yourself there one day. When the opportunity came knocking on my door I didn't look like someone that could travel to the United Kingdom to study but because I was prepared, the opportunity had no choice but to take me along with it.

An opportunity is coming that will take you abroad and to places and heights you never thought you could reach, just get prepared for it.

My desire is to see you succeed.

See you at the top.

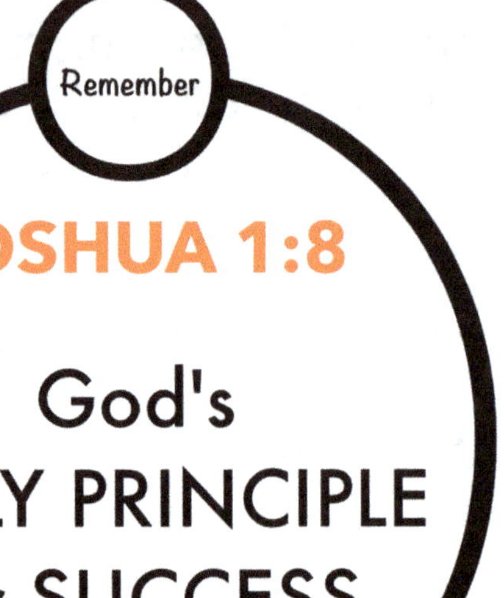

Remember
JOSHUA 1:8
God's
ONLY PRINCIPLE
for SUCCESS

Please keep in touch.

It would be a great pleasure to hear from you.

Email: contactogan@gmail.com

To order copies of this book please contact the author via the number +234 8109670769